CW00661714

SEX TIPS

FOR HUSBANDS
& WIVES
FROM 1894

SEX TIPS FOR HUSBANDS AND WIVES

First published in 2008
This edition copyright © Summersdale Publishers Ltd, 2014

Summersdale Publishers Ltd
46 West Street
Chichester
West Sussex
PO19 1RP
UK

www.summersdale.com

Printed and bound in the Czech Republic

ISBN: 978-1-84953-573-1

Substantial discounts on bulk quantities of Summersdale books
are available to corporations, professional associations and other
organisations. For details contact Nicky Douglas by telephone:
+44 (0) 1243 756902, fax: +44 (0) 1243 786300 or email:
nicky@summersdale.com.

SEX TIPS

FOR HUSBANDS
& WIVES
FROM 1894

RUTH SMYTHERS

INSTRUCTION
AND ADVICE
FOR THE YOUNG BRIDE

on the Conduct and
Procedure of the Intimate
and Personal Relationships
of the Marriage State
for the Greater Spiritual
Sanctity of this
Blessed Sacrament
and the Glory of God

by
Ruth Smythers
beloved wife of
The Reverend L. D. Smythers
Pastor of the Arcadian
Methodist Church of the
Eastern Regional Conference
Published in the year
of our Lord 1894
Spiritual Guidance Press
New York City

To the sensitive young woman
who has had the benefits
of proper upbringing, the
wedding day is, ironically,
both the happiest and most
terrifying day of her life.

On the positive side, there
is the wedding itself, in
which the bride is the central
attraction in a beautiful and
inspiring ceremony...

... symbolising her triumph
in securing a male to provide
for all her needs for the
rest of her life.

On the negative side, there
is the wedding night, during
which the bride must pay
the piper, so to speak, by
facing for the first time the
terrible experience of sex.

At this point, dear reader,
let me concede one
shocking truth.

Some young women actually
anticipate the wedding night
ordeal with curiosity and
pleasure! Beware such
an attitude!

A selfish and sensual husband
can easily take advantage of
such a bride. One cardinal
rule of marriage should
never be forgotten:

GIVE LITTLE,
GIVE SELDOM,
AND ABOVE ALL,
GIVE GRUDGINGLY.

Otherwise what could have
been a proper marriage
could become an orgy of
sexual lust.

On the other hand, the
bride's terror need not be
extreme. While sex is at best
revolting and at worst
rather painful...

... it has to be endured, and
has been by women since
the beginning of time, and
is compensated for by the
monogamous home and by the
children produced through it.

It is useless, in most cases,
for the bride to prevail upon
the groom to forego the
sexual initiation.

While the ideal husband would
be one who would approach
his bride only at her request
and only for the purpose of
begetting offspring, such
nobility and unselfishness
cannot be expected from
the average man.

Most men, if not denied,
would demand sex
almost every day.

The wise bride will permit
a maximum of two brief
sexual experiences weekly
during the first months
of marriage.

As time goes by she should
make every effort to
reduce this frequency.

Feigned illness, sleepiness,
and headaches are among
the wife's best friends
in this matter.

Arguments, nagging, scolding, and bickering also prove very effective, if used in the late evening about an hour before the husband would normally commence his seduction.

Clever wives are ever on
the alert for new and better
methods of denying and
discouraging the amorous
overtures of the husband.

A good wife should expect to
have reduced sexual contacts
to once a week by the end of
the first year of marriage and
to once a month by the end
of the fifth year of marriage.

By their tenth anniversary
many wives have managed
to complete their child
bearing and have achieved the
ultimate goal of terminating
all sexual contacts with
the husband.

By this time she can depend
upon his love for the
children and social pressures
to hold the husband
in the home.

Just as she should be ever
alert to keep the quantity of
sex as low as possible, the
wise bride will pay equal
attention to limiting the
kind and degree of
sexual contacts.

Most men are by nature
rather perverted, and if given
half a chance, would engage
in quite a variety of the
most revolting practices.

These practices include, among others: performing the normal act in abnormal positions; mouthing the female body; and offering their own vile bodies to be mouthed in turn.

Nudity, talking about
sex, reading stories about
sex, viewing photographs
and drawings depicting
or suggesting sex are the
obnoxious habits the male is
likely to acquire if permitted.

A wise bride will make it
the goal never to allow her
husband to see her unclothed
body, and never allow him
to display his unclothed
body to her.

Sex, when it cannot be
prevented, should be
practised only in
total darkness.

Many women have found it
useful to have thick cotton
nightgowns for themselves and
pajamas for their husbands.
These should be donned in
separate rooms. They need
not be removed during the
sex act. Thus, a minimum
of flesh is exposed.

Once the bride has donned
her gown and turned off
all the lights, she should lie
quietly upon the bed and
await her groom. When he
comes groping into the room
she should make no sound to
guide him in her direction,
lest he take this as a sign
of encouragement.

She should let him grope in
the dark. There is always the
hope that he will stumble
and incur some slight injury
which she can use as an excuse
to deny him sexual access.

When he finds her, the wife
should lie as still as possible.
Bodily motion on her part
could be interpreted as
sexual excitement by the
optimistic husband.

If he attempts to kiss her
on the lips she should turn
her head slightly so that the
kiss falls harmlessly on her
cheek instead.

If he attempts to kiss her
hand, she should make a fist.

If he lifts her gown and
attempts to kiss her any place
else she should quickly pull
the gown back in place, spring
from the bed, and announce
that nature calls her
to the toilet.

This will generally dampen
his desire to kiss in the
forbidden territory.

If the husband attempts to
seduce her with lascivious talk,
the wise wife will suddenly
remember some trivial non-
sexual question to ask him.

MENU

Once he answers she should
keep the conversation going,
no matter how frivolous
it may seem at the time.

TIME FLIES

Eventually, the husband
will learn that if he insists
on having sexual contact, he
must get on with it without
amorous embellishment.

The wise wife will allow
him to pull the gown up no
farther than the waist, and
only permit him to open
the front of his pajamas to
thus make connection.

She will be absolutely silent or
babble about her housework
while he is huffing and puffing
away. Above all, she will lie
perfectly still and never under
any circumstances grunt
or groan while the act is
in progress.

As soon as the husband has
completed the act, the wise
wife will start nagging him
about various minor tasks
she wishes him to perform
on the morrow.

Many men obtain a major
portion of their sexual
satisfaction from the peaceful
exhaustion immediately
after the act is over.

Thus the wife must insure that there is no peace in this period for him to enjoy. Otherwise, he might be encouraged to soon try for more.

One heartening factor for which the wife can be grateful is the fact that the husband's home, school, church, and social environment have been working together all through his life to instil in him a deep sense of guilt in regards to his sexual feelings...

... so that he comes to
the marriage couch
apologetically and filled
with shame, already half
cowed and subdued.

The wise wife seizes upon
this advantage and relentlessly
pursues her goal first to limit,
later to annihilate completely
her husband's desire for
sexual expression.

If you're interested in finding
out more about our books,
find us on Facebook at
Summersdale Publishers
and follow us on Twitter
at **@Summersdale**.

www.summersdale.com